Profiles in American History

The Life and Times of

ALEXANDER HAMILTON

Mitchell Lane
PUBLISHERS

P.O. Box 196 · Hockessin, Delaware 19707

Titles in the Series

The Life and Times of

Profiles in American History

The Life and Times of

ALEXANDER
HAMILTON

Russell Roberts

Printing   1   2   3   4   5   6   7   8   9

Library of Congress Cataloging-in-Publication Data
Roberts, Russell.
    The life and times of Alexander Hamilton/by Russell Roberts.
        p. cm. — (Profiles in American history)
    Includes bibliographical references and index.
    ISBN 1-58415-436-5 (library bound: alk. paper)
    1. Hamilton, Alexander 1757-1804—Juvenile literature. 2. Statesmen—United States—Biography—Juvenile literature. 3. United States—History—Revolution, 1775–1783—Juvenile literature. 4. United States—Politics and government—1783–1809—Juvenile literature. I. Title. II. Series.
E302.6 H2R595 2006
973.4'092—dc22
                                       2005028506
ISBN-10: 1-58415-436-5   ISBN-13:978-1-58415-436-5

ABOUT THE AUTHOR: Russell Roberts has written and published nearly 40 books for adults and children on a variety of subjects, including baseball, memory power, business, New Jersey history, and travel. The lives of American figures of distinction is a particular area of interest for him. He has written numerous books for Mitchell Lane, including *Pedro Menendez de Aviles, Philo Farnsworth Invents TV, Robert Goddard, Bernardo de Galvez,* and *Where Did the Dinosaurs Go?* He lives in Bordentown, New Jersey, with his family and a fat, fuzzy, and crafty calico cat named Rusti.

PHOTO CREDITS: Cover, pp. 1, 3: Library of Congress; p. 6: Getty Images; p. 10: Library of Congress; p. 13: Jamie Kondrchek; p. 16, 19, 21: Library of Congress; p. 24: Corbis; p. 27: Library of Congress; p. 30; Corbis; pp. 32, 35, 39: Library of Congress

PUBLISHER'S NOTE: This story is based on the author's extensive research, which he believes to be accurate. Documentation of such research is contained on page 46.
    The internet sites referenced herein were active as of the publication date. Due to the fleeting nature of some web sites, we cannot guarantee they will all be active when you are reading this book.
                                                    PLB

Profiles in American History

Contents

An artist's idea of the duel between Alexander Hamilton and Vice President Aaron Burr. As the United States was forming, the paths of Hamilton and Burr crossed many times.

CHAPTER 1

Duel at Dawn

Early Wednesday morning, July 11, 1804, three men climbed into a small boat at William Bayard's dock on the New York side of the Hudson River. When everyone was settled, the boatman's oars dipped into the water. The boat headed for New Jersey.

The sun shone brightly overhead as the boat slowly made its way across the sparkling river. The day had dawned cool and pleasant. A few birds flew overhead. As the river slowly awakened, the boatman's oars splashed in the water.

The three men in the boat were quiet. Each was lost in thought. One of the men, Alexander Hamilton, had been an important aide to General George Washington during the American Revolution. He had also been the first Treasury Secretary of the United States. He had established a new financial system for the young country. Now he was going to fight a duel . . . perhaps to the death.

The other two men in the boat were Hamilton's long-time friend Nathaniel Pendleton and Dr. David Hosack. Pendleton was Hamilton's second in the duel. A second was like an assistant for the duelist.

The New Jersey shoreline was near. The boat landed close to the village of Weehawken. Hamilton and Pendleton got out. Hosack and the boatman remained with the boat.

The two men walked up a steep, narrow path until they reached an open area of ground surrounded by trees. Waiting for them there were Aaron Burr, the vice president of the United States, and William Van Ness, Burr's second.

Hamilton and Burr nodded at each other. Their seconds gave each man a pistol. Hamilton raised his pistol to test the light, then pulled out a pair of spectacles and put them on. There was a moment's quiet, then either Pendleton or Van Ness yelled, "Present."[1]

There were two shots. Hamilton's apparently went into the trees. Burr's shot struck Hamilton in the right side, just above the hip. It hit one of Hamilton's ribs, struck his liver, and shattered one of the vertebrae of his spinal column. He pitched forward and fell to the ground.

Pendleton rushed to Hamilton. He turned him over, put his arms around him, and pulled him to a half-sitting position under a tree. Burr moved toward Hamilton, but Van Ness told him to leave.

Pendleton called for Hosack. The doctor rushed up the path, brushing past Burr coming down. Van Ness was concealing Burr's face with an umbrella, so Hosack did not notice him.

Hosack reached the clearing and hurried over to Hamilton. "This is a mortal wound, Doctor,"[2] Hamilton gasped. Silently the doctor agreed. He thought that Hamilton might die at any moment.

Hosack and Pendleton carried the stricken man back to the river. The boatman helped put Hamilton into the boat. Then he placed the case with Hamilton's dueling pistol beside him. The former Treasury Secretary's eyes were closed. His breathing was raspy.

As the boat headed back toward New York, the doctor worked on Hamilton. He massaged his face, lips, arms, and chest with spirits of hartshorn, which was then used as a stimulant. The combination of the vigorous massage, the hartshorn, and the cool breeze revived Hamilton. He half-opened his eyes and said, "My vision is indistinct."[3] As he got stronger, his eyesight returned.

Once his vision had come back, Hamilton saw the case with the dueling pistol in the boat. "Take care of that pistol—it is cocked! [ready to be fired]" Hamilton urged. "It may go off and do mischief."[4] A few minutes later, Hamilton said, "Pendleton knows that I did not intend to fire at him."[5]

Those two statements by Hamilton helped ignite a historical controversy that continues today. Did he or did he not try to shoot at Burr? If he did, why did he say what he did to his friend? Furthermore, why was Hamilton so worried when he saw the pistol? Was he assuming that it was still loaded? Would he have thought that if he had tried to shoot Burr? But if he had no intention of shooting at Burr, why did he fight the duel at all? Why did his dueling pistol have a special hair trigger that could be easily fired?

These are questions that only Alexander Hamilton could have answered. But he was silent as his boat moved toward the New York shoreline. Maybe he was thinking about his amazing life. . . .

Aaron Burr

Aaron Burr

Aaron Burr was born in Newark, New Jersey, on February 6, 1756. His mother's name was Esther. His father, the Reverend Aaron Burr, was the president of the College of New Jersey (now Princeton). Aaron was a sickly baby; he almost died twice when he was very young. By the time he was around two years old, his parents both died, and he went to live with his uncle Timothy Edwards in Elizabethtown, New Jersey. Edwards beat young Aaron, several times causing the boy to try to run away from home.

Burr entered Princeton at age thirteen, and graduated from there with distinction in 1772, at sixteen years old. The Revolutionary War started while he was in law school, and in 1775 he joined the Colonial Army. He retired four years later for health reasons.

Burr was appointed attorney general of New York in 1789; he served as a senator from that state from 1791 to 1797. In 1800 he ran with Thomas Jefferson of the Republican Party (which is the ancestor of today's Democratic Party) for the presidency. At this time, the man who got the most electoral votes was to be the president, and the one with the second-most the vice president. The other candidates were current President John Adams and his running mate, Charles Pinckney. Jefferson and Burr both finished ahead of Adams and Pinckney. Burr was clearly supposed to be the vice presidential choice, but when he got the same number of electoral votes as Jefferson, the election was thrown to the House of Representatives, where it was rumored that Burr was trying to make a political deal to become president. However, Hamilton's support of Jefferson helped swing him the election. The Republicans, angry with Burr for almost stealing the presidency from Jefferson, did not want him back in 1804. Burr then lost the New York governor's race. He felt that he had lost largely because of Hamilton's continued attacks on him. Eventually, Burr's injured feelings led him to challenge Hamilton to a duel.

The duel finished Burr's political career. He then got involved in a mysterious scheme involving the Louisiana Territory, Spain, and the United States. He was arrested for treason, but was acquitted in 1807. Never able to make people forget the famous duel, Burr died in 1836.

For Your Information

When Alexander Hamilton was just 16 years old, he was left in charge of the leading import/export company on St. Croix. His quick mind was so impressive, a visiting clergyman arranged a scholarship for Hamilton to go to college in New York.

CHAPTER
2

A Boy Alone

Mary Fawcett (or Faucett) and her daughter Rachel lived on Nevis, a small West Indian island. Nevis is one of a group of islands in the Lesser Antilles, which form an arc that separates the Caribbean Sea from the Atlantic Ocean.

Christopher Columbus named Nevis from the Spanish phrase Nuestra Señora de Las Nieves, meaning "Our Lady of the Snows." The large cloud around Nevis's mountain reminded him of snow, but Nevis's climate is actually hot and humid.

In 1741, eleven-year-old Rachel and her mother moved to the nearby island of St. Croix. Six years later, a sugar plantation owner named Johann Levine (also spelled Lavine, Lavien, Lowein, and Levin) met Rachel. They got married, but the two were not happy. Miserable, she tried to run away. At this time in history, women had few rights. Levine had Rachel put in jail. She was soon freed and returned with her mother to Nevis.

On Nevis, Rachel met Scotsman James Hamilton. They began living together, although she was still legally married to Levine. She was 21, and Hamilton was 32. They had two sons. The first, James, was born in 1753. The second, Alexander, was born on January 11, 1755, in a large house opposite a church in Charlestown, Nevis.

Alexander grew up among the island's sugarcane plantations. He breathed the fresh air, walked in fields of sweet potatoes, and swam

in the crystal-clear blue-green water. Since sugarcane plantations used slave labor, he also saw firsthand the cruelty of slavery.

In 1765 Hamilton left Rachel and his two children. Alexander always expected him to return, but he never saw his father again.

On her own, Rachel returned to St. Croix, opened a small store, and struggled to support herself and two children. In February 1768, at 39 years old, Rachel died of yellow fever. Suddenly, James and Alexander were all alone.

Initially young Alexander got some help from his mother's relatives. Then they too died, and he was again alone. Fortunately he was living with the family of a friend named Edward Stevens, who gave him food and shelter. In his small room at the Stevens house, Alexander read the books his mother had left him. Soon he was quite knowledgeable.

Hamilton got a job as a clerk with the import/export company Beekman and Cruger. They were the leading St. Croix exporter of sugar and molasses to America, and a major importer of food. Hamilton was good at his work. In October 1771, when company head Nicholas Cruger got sick and went to New York for treatment, he put the pale, sixteen-year-old, red-haired boy in charge of the business. When he returned in March 1772, his business was as healthy as—if not even healthier than—it was the day he left.

Around this time the Reverend Hugh Knox arrived on St. Croix. Hamilton impressed him. Knox knew Hamilton needed to leave the tiny island to continue his education. He arranged a scholarship for Hamilton so that he could go to college in New York City in America. In October 1772, Hamilton boarded a ship for America, carrying a trunk containing extra clothes and his precious books. He never returned to the West Indies.

In late October, Hamilton arrived in Boston. The changing autumn leaves fascinated him. Shortly, he went to New York, whose population of 20,000 was greater than all of St. Croix. He sought out the Reverend John Rogers, who was supposed to try to get him into the College of New Jersey (now called Princeton). Hamilton's limited schooling worried Rogers. Rogers suggested he go to Elizabethtown Academy for one year to catch up on his studies.

Elizabethtown Academy was located in today's city of Elizabeth, New Jersey. It was a prep school, meaning that it helped prepare

Alexander Hamilton was born on the tiny island of Nevis in the Lesser Antilles. Nevis is only seven miles long. There were very few opportunities to get a good education there. Saint Croix, where his mother opened a store, is in the Virgin Islands, just east of Puerto Rico.

young men for college. Anxious to go to college, Hamilton decided to complete all the courses that he needed—about three years' worth—in less than one year. He studied from early morning until late at night. He was often found in the graveyard next to the academy, leaning against a tombstone and reading a book.

While at Elizabethtown he met some of the leaders of the growing American revolutionary movement, such as William Livingston, Elias Boudinot, and John Jay. Hamilton enjoyed his time at the academy. In the winter, he went sledding or skated on frozen ponds

or lakes. In nicer weather, he took horseback rides to William Livingston's house.

After he successfully completed his studies at Elizabethtown in June 1773, Hamilton applied to Princeton. The college president rejected his demand that his admission be on the same accelerated basis as at Elizabethtown. So Hamilton applied to King's College in New York City—now called Columbia University—which accepted his demand.

Hamilton fit right in to New York City. It was a quickly growing city with a great mixture of people, including Irish, Scot, German, English, and French. Born in the British West Indies, Hamilton felt almost like a native there.

Ironically, Hamilton favored the British side over the colonies when he first arrived in America, but he soon switched allegiance. He began writing pamphlets defending the colonists.

In the spring of 1774, several months after the Boston Tea Party, a ship carrying British tea, the *London,* arrived in New York Harbor. Patriot leaders from the city, perhaps including Hamilton, handed out "invitations" to their own "tea party" aboard the *London.* But the large group of protesters that gathered could not be controlled. The ship's captain and crew barely escaped with their lives. Hamilton was horrified at the fury of an uncontrolled mob.

". . . while the passions of men are worked up to an uncommon pitch," Hamilton said about mob action, "there is a great danger of fatal extremes."[1]

In the autumn and winter of 1774–75, Hamilton led two lives. By day he was apparently a loyal King's College student. By night he was writing pamphlets for publication that supported the American cause. In those days a person would choose a fake name—known as a pen name—under which to write and publish political writings. Hamilton's pen names, historians believe, included Americanus and Monitor.

Alexander Hamilton had found a cause. He was no longer a boy alone.

The Uncertain Truth

Alexander Hamilton

Exact dates in history are sometimes hard to pinpoint. This is certainly the case with Alexander Hamilton. Biographers and historians differ about the exact years that some of the people in his life, including Hamilton himself, were born. In fact, there is even a dispute about who his father was!

The year of Hamilton's birth is given as 1755 or 1757. Sources also disagree on the birth order of him and his brother James. Alexander is usually portrayed as his mother's younger son, but some claim that he was several years older than James.

Figuring out who Hamilton's real father was gets even trickier. James Hamilton is the person usually credited, but others claim his father was Thomas Stevens of St. Croix, father of his lifelong friend Ned Stevens. (Would this account for why the Stevens family took him in after his mother's death?) Supposedly the two looked extremely similar. Other sources claim Hamilton's father was a British official named William Leslie Hamilton. Some even claim that his real father was George Washington!

Another disagreement concerns the day that Hamilton married. Some sources give the date as December 14; others, December 17.

There is also disagreement about how many of the famous essays known as the Federalist Papers were written by Hamilton. Some credit him with 51 of the essays. The essays, which number 85 in all, argued for the ratification of the U.S. Constitution. The essays were written anonymously, with the writers using pen names to disguise their true identity—though we now know that Hamilton, James Madison, and John Jay were the authors. How many did Hamilton write? While it would certainly make historians happy to find out the exact answer, the truth is that no one knows, and no one will probably ever know. Sometimes in history, it is hard to find "the truth."

For Your Information

An artist's idea of the Battle of Lexington. Thanks to the efforts of Paul Revere and William Dawes, when the British Redcoats marched on Lexington, the colonists were ready to return their fire. The battles of Lexington and Concord were renowned as "the shot heard 'round the world."

CHAPTER
3

Washington's Right Hand

In April 1775, the war that neither side wanted but both seemed powerless to prevent began. Armed groups of colonists and British soldiers fought at the battles of Lexington and Concord in Massachusetts, sparking the American Revolution.

Shortly thereafter, Hamilton began drilling with a militia company he formed. They drilled every morning in a churchyard. They wore green coats and leather caps that read "Freedom or Death."

The revolution came home to Hamilton on May 10, 1775. He was awakened in his room at King's College by the noise of a large crowd outside. As he leaned out his window, he saw that an angry mob had gathered at the college fence. They wanted to tar and feather the Reverend Myles Cooper, the president of King's College and a noted British sympathizer. Rushing downstairs, Hamilton stood in front of the crowd and tried to talk them out of it. The delay gave Cooper enough time to escape out a back door.

On June 25, Hamilton stood in a crowd with eight other militia companies as the new commander of the Colonial Army, George Washington, inspected them. Little did Hamilton realize how important a role Washington was to play in his life.

In January 1776, Hamilton learned that an artillery company was being formed for the defense of New York against the British. He applied for command of the company, even though he was young and

had just come to New York a few years before. In March, he became Captain Alexander Hamilton, head of the Provincial Company of Artillery of New York. He took his scholarship money, had a uniform made, and never returned to college.

On July 4, 1776, Hamilton watched with his men on Bayard's Hill in lower Manhattan as British ships began unloading the first of what would ultimately be 39,000 troops onto Staten Island. When they struck on August 27, they attacked 10,000 American troops in Brooklyn Heights. The American forces there were overwhelmed. Hamilton stayed in Manhattan, with other troops, while Washington got most of his defeated army safely out of the city. In early September, Hamilton and the rest of the colonial troops hurriedly evacuated the rest of the city to avoid capture. They left so quickly that Hamilton could take only the clothes he was wearing and his horse.

By December, Washington had taken notice of Hamilton. He was reportedly "charmed by the brilliant courage"[1] Hamilton displayed. Hamilton's actions were one of the few bright spots for Washington and the colonials that winter. The army was cold, hungry, and depressed. Washington decided on a bold move: to attack the Hessians at Trenton, New Jersey. Hamilton and his men were among those who crossed the icy Delaware River on Christmas night to surprise the Hessian troops. During the battle, it was Hamilton's artillery that helped seal the victory for the Americans by stopping the Hessians from organizing a counterattack.

Several days later the Americans won another victory. Hamilton's artillery again played an important part in the battle. According to legend, one of his cannonballs smashed through a window at Princeton College and beheaded a portrait of England's King George II.

The two victories brought new volunteers into the army and boosted the American cause. Washington, getting busier all the time, needed help. Already impressed by Hamilton, in January 1777 he asked him to join his staff. Hamilton was promoted from captain to lieutenant colonel at the age of twenty-two.

Thus began a relationship between the two men that lasted the rest of their lives. Washington soon grew to trust Hamilton. In turn, the young officer became Washington's strong right hand. Hamilton made decisions and gave orders with confidence because he knew that he had Washington's support.

Seasoned officers from Germany, Poland, and France contributed a great deal to America's success in the Revolutionary War. Here Washington is painted with officers Baron de Kalb, Baron von Steuben, Kazimierz Pulaski, Thaddeus Kosciusko, and Marquis de Lafayette.

"He made more suggestions than anyone else on the headquarters staff, but then he also relieved Washington of more numerous burdens by writing and acting on his own orders,"[2] writes Hamilton biographer Willard Randall.

In the winter of 1777–78, as the American army shivered at Valley Forge, Hamilton helped put down a movement by several politicians and officers to get rid of Washington and place General Horatio Gates in command. The American Revolution may have ended quite differently without Washington in command.

In the spring of 1778, Hamilton welcomed a German officer named Baron von Steuben to Valley Forge. Von Steuben spent many hours training the American soldiers and turning them into an army capable of standing up to the British. Hamilton helped von Steuben with many things, such as writing a new manual of arms with which to practice drilling.

As Washington's aide, Hamilton had a front-row seat to the workings of the Continental Congress. He was not pleased with what he saw. He was critical of the Congress for not supplying enough food, clothing, and other supplies to assist the army. These feelings would resurface later in Hamilton's advocacy for a strong central executive.

Hamilton also began speaking against slavery. Most likely he recalled the cruelty of slavery from his youth. Together with another officer, he worked out a plan to offer freedom to any slaves in South Carolina who would fight against the British. At that time, many people felt that African-Americans would not make good soldiers. Hamilton disagreed.

"I have not the least doubt that the Negroes will make very excellent soldiers,"[3] he wrote.

Hamilton was an aggressive soldier. He became annoyed when Washington's generals voted to merely harass the British Army with just a few thousand troops, rather than attack them as they crossed New Jersey in June 1778 on their way to New York City. The decision "would have done honor to the most honorable society of midwives, and to them only,"[4] he wrote sarcastically.

The harassment turned into a major battle when the British Army responded with a full-scale attack. In the ensuing Battle of Monmouth, New Jersey, Hamilton was everywhere, riding back and forth across the field as bullets whizzed by him. He helped stop the colonials, under the command of General Charles Lee, from retreating under the British onslaught. Soon Washington arrived and personally took command, rallying the army and leading the Americans to a draw. The Battle of Monmouth is considered one of the turning points of the war. If Hamilton had not been there to help stop the Americans' initial retreat, there is a good chance the outcome of the war would have been different.

During the battle, Hamilton was seriously injured when his horse was shot and fell on top of him. A week later, he had recovered

Benedict Arnold was a colonial officer who secretly plotted with the British against the Americans. Hamilton chased Arnold when his treason was discovered, but he could not catch him.

enough to be the key witness in the court-martial of General Charles Lee. It was Hamilton's testimony in favor of Washington and against Lee that got Lee tossed out of the army. Listening with quiet anger to Hamilton was one of Lee's officers—Lieutenant Colonel Aaron Burr.

Hamilton's defense of Washington made him many enemies. He was criticized because of his foreign birth. His enemies said that someone who was not born in America could not possibly want to fight hard for its freedom. It was whispered that Hamilton was just terribly ambitious, and wanted to make sure that he was going to get a high political office if America won.

The winter of 1779–1780 was another brutal one for the Colonial Army. Hamilton, however, may not have noticed the cold. He was courting twenty-three-year-old Elizabeth "Betsy" Schuyler, the daughter of Philip Schuyler, one of the wealthiest men in America. Betsy was an artist and outdoorswoman who could speak French and Dutch as well as she could English. By the spring of 1780, the two were engaged to be married. "Though not a genius, she has good sense enough to be agreeable, and though not a beauty, she has fine black eyes,"[5] Hamilton said about her.

Hamilton and Betsy were married in December 1780. (The date is often given as either December 14 or December 17.) Some think that he married her because of her father's wealth, especially given his feeling that "money is an essential ingredient to happiness in this world."[6] But he certainly cared for her. He spent much of the summer and fall before the wedding thinking about Betsy. "You are certainly a little sorceress and have bewitched me,"[7] he told her.

In the fall of 1780, Hamilton found himself at yet another turning point in the American Revolution. On the morning of September 25, he and another officer pursued American General Benedict Arnold, who was secretly working with the British, but they did not catch him. Arnold's treachery stunned Washington. It was Hamilton who helped Washington weather the crisis.

Even as Washington relied more heavily on Hamilton, the young officer was upset at being stuck at headquarters, far away from battlefield action. He yearned for the chance to win honor and glory under fire. Finally, on February 16, 1781, Hamilton and Washington had a silly argument. After telling Hamilton that he wanted to speak to him, Washington felt that Hamilton had left him waiting too long. "You treat me with disrespect,"[8] the general angrily said to his aide.

"I am not conscious of it, sir, but since you have thought it necessary to tell me so, we must part,"[9] Hamilton replied.

So two men who had been absolutely essential to the American war effort parted company. In the years that he had served Washington, Hamilton had been in the middle of many important events, and had made many critical decisions that impacted the future of the war. In the process, the boy had become a man. On May 30, 1781, as he formally resigned as Washington's aide and rode away from the army, Alexander Hamilton had to be wondering what life next held for him.

The Battle of Monmouth

The Battle of Monmouth was one of the turning points of the American Revolution. It was fought on June 28, 1778, in the town of Freehold, New Jersey.

The British Army had evacuated Philadelphia and was retreating across New Jersey toward New York. Washington ordered General Charles Lee to attack the rear of the British Army. Expecting little resistance, Lee was unprepared when the entire force

General Charles Lee

turned around and started to fight. Lee quickly ordered a retreat.

Washington, also expecting an easy victory, ate a leisurely breakfast that morning at the home of Dr. James English before heading for the battlefield. Thus he was shocked to see his troops retreating.

Angrily, Washington rode forward to confront Lee. Lee was expecting to be congratulated on the way he had saved the outnumbered American troops from being overrun, and thus he was surprised by Washington's anger. According to legend, Washington swore at him so violently that it shook the leaves on nearby trees. Washington relieved Lee, took command, and rallied the American forces to a draw. That night, the British Army abandoned the field and retreated to Sandy Hook.

The Battle of Monmouth lasted from dawn until midnight—the longest sustained battle in history up to that point. It was the last major fight of the American Revolution between British and American troops in the north of America. Although technically a draw, the battle was important because it boosted colonial morale and increased support for the war. It also showed the Americans that they could stand toe-to-toe with the mighty British Army, which at that time was considered the best army in the world. The battle also resulted in Lee's being court-martialed and subsequently kicked out of the army.

For Your Information

Elizabeth "Betsy" Schuyler married
Alexander Hamilton in December of 1780.
She outlived her husband by fifty years,
and was a staunch defender of his work
and reputation until the day she died.

CHAPTER 4

Constitutional Advocate

For a while after leaving the army, Hamilton stayed with his wife's family. Betsy was pregnant, his father-in-law ill, and Hamilton's presence seemed necessary. While he was at the Schuyler home, he wrote out his views on an ideal new American government. He discussed the need for a strong central government and a national bank. Above all, he noted the need for money to accomplish things. He felt strongly that the individual states had to give Congress the means to raise money.

"Power without revenue is a bubble,"[1] he wrote. He meant that if Congress did not have the right to raise money through taxation and other means, then the national government (as represented by Congress) would be powerless. Hamilton was forming the ideas that he would eventually use to establish the future economic system of the United States of America. As biographer Willard Randall noted, "[F]rom that time on, no American of the Revolutionary generation spent more of his thoughts, words, and time to win over the common citizen to an energetic national government."[2]

Still he pestered Washington for a field command leading troops. Finally the general allowed Hamilton to command a battalion heading to Yorktown, Virginia. On October 14, 1781, Hamilton and his men risked their lives in a successful attack on a key enemy position. The American triumph at Yorktown effectively ended the war.

Hamilton returned to life with his wife at her father's house. He became a member of the New York congressional delegation, and studied law. On January 22, 1782, Betsy gave birth to the couple's first son, Philip. They would have seven more children.

Hamilton studied hard for the law, using the books in his father-in-law's vast library. One other person was also using Philip Schuyler's books to study: Colonel Aaron Burr.

Hamilton was appointed to Congress in July 1782 and took his seat on November 25. The next few years were not good ones for the new American nation. Trying to operate under the weak Articles of Confederation, in which most of the power rested with the individual states, the country had many problems. Chief among them was the nation's growing debt. States refused to pay taxes, and Congress could only ask—not require—them to pay. Some states had financed their own military operations during the war. They were demanding that Congress pay for those. With little money in the treasury, Congress was months behind in payments to army veterans. Payments were also due to foreign countries that had loaned America money during the war.

The fiscal mess did have one good result: It healed the rift between Hamilton and Washington. Washington told Hamilton that he shared his opinion about a stronger central government: "For it is clearly my opinion [that] unless Congress have powers competent to all general purposes, that the distresses we have encountered, the expenses we have incurred, and the blood we have spilled in the course of an eight years' war will avail us nothing."[3]

Finally, in June 1783, over 100 army veterans, angered because they had not been paid, marched on the Congress in Philadelphia, demanding their money. Congress fled to Princeton. Hamilton was again in the middle of the controversy, making arrangements to pay the veterans while also seeing to the safety of Congress.

In late 1783, Hamilton moved his family into a house at No. 57 Wall Street in New York City. He set up a law practice in a rented office next door.

On January 25, 1785, Hamilton and his friend Hercules Mulligan established the Society for Promoting the Manumission [freedom] of Slaves in New York. Unlike many of the other Founding Fathers, Hamilton never owned a slave. (However, he could never convince

British troops surrender to the Americans after the Battle of Yorktown, ending the American Revolution.

his wife to give up her one slave.) He remembered the horror of slavery from his boyhood, calling it "a commerce so repugnant to humanity."[4] At a time when freeing the slaves and abolishing slavery was not an issue for many Americans, Hamilton was one of the first prominent men to bring the idea out into the open.

Another unpopular idea that Hamilton took on was treatment of Americans who had remained loyal to England during the Revolution. Not everyone in America had sided with the Patriots. Now the Loyalists, as they were called, were being attacked by mobs, tarred and feathered, and run out of town. However, many Loyalists had wealth and property. Hamilton was afraid that making Loyalists flee the city, or even the country, would seriously weaken both the state and national economies. Even though he had just risked his life in a war against the British, he spoke out against mistreatment of those who had been loyal to Britain. Between 1784 and 1791, he defended over sixty Loyalists. Eventually, because of Hamilton, New York became the first state to restore full civil rights to Loyalists.

By 1786, Hamilton was the leading lawyer in New York. Besides taking cases that other attorneys would not, he also was the leading lawyer for business interests.

In 1784, Frenchman and Revolutionary War hero Marquis de Lafayette returned to America for a visit. Together, he and Hamilton helped found the Society of the Cincinnati for former officers of the American army during the Revolution. Among other things, the society provided financial aid to the officers. Hamilton himself gave Baron von Steuben about $27,000 over four years when von Steuben was having financial difficulties.

While his political and legal career were going well, Hamilton's personal life was not. Betsy liked neither the crowded city nor its busy nightlife. She was shy and was often sick. Her frequent pregnancies added to her discomfort. She preferred staying at the Albany estate of her parents in upper New York. Hamilton was often alone.

He began seeing more and more of Betsy's sister, Angelica. She was more outgoing and friendlier than Betsy, and liked the social whirl of parties and balls—just like Hamilton. Her husband, John Church, went to England for long periods of time for business and politics, leaving his wife behind. His head, wrote Angelica Church sadly, "is full of politics. . . . I am no longer heard."[5]

Eventually, some believe, these two lonely people became romantically involved with each other. They worked out an affectionate code in their letters that was so subtle that some historians still don't know if Betsy knew that her sister and her husband were involved. Others, however, say there is little doubt that Betsy knew of her husband and sister's attraction to each other. The full extent of their relationship will probably never be known.

Hamilton continued to try to make Betsy happy. He bought No. 57 Wall Street, the rented building in which they lived, so that Betsy would consider the home hers. He also bought the building next door. Incidentally, Aaron Burr represented the building's seller.

Meanwhile, the new nation that Hamilton had fought so hard for was tottering on the brink of disaster. Lack of revenue and real political power plagued the Congress. Hamilton knew that something must be done. While attending a commercial convention of the states in Annapolis, Maryland, in September 1786, he called for a convention in Philadelphia the following May to fix the governing system. "There are important defects in the system of the Federal government,"[6] he said.

But would the May convention come too late? Daniel Shays, a poor farmer in western Massachusetts, was having trouble paying his debts and was at risk of losing his property. In the autumn of 1786, he gathered over 1,000 armed men in similar situations and started a short-lived rebellion against poor economic conditions.

"We are fast verging to anarchy and confusion,"[7] said George Washington.

Fortunately, the fragile fabric of the nation held together. On May 18, 1787, Hamilton arrived in Philadelphia on a summer-like day and checked into the Indian Queen Tavern on Third Street. The Constitutional Convention at Independence Hall was about to start.

Hamilton was just over thirty years old—less than half the age of many delegates. He was in a room with such brilliant minds as Benjamin Franklin, James Madison, and Gouverneur Morris. For the first few weeks Hamilton listened as the convention debated several plans for a new American government. One plan was just a revision of the feeble Articles of Confederation. Another went far beyond that and proposed an entirely new form of governmental structure. Silently Hamilton sat at the table for the New York delegates, letting others speak while he listened.

Then, early in the June 18th session, Hamilton asked convention president Washington for the floor. The tall, youthful New Yorker then spoke for five straight hours.

Hamilton began by noting that the current crisis in the country "was too serious to permit any scruples whatever to prevail over the duty imposed on every man to contribute his efforts for the public safety and happiness."[8]

He criticized the government plans put forth so far, especially the one that retained the Articles of Confederation. He laid the current troubles with the American government at the doorstep of the states: ". . . no amendment of the Confederation can answer the purpose of a good government, so long as the state sovereignties do, in any shape, exist,"[9] he said.

He favored "extinguishing"[10] (lessening the power of) the state governments. "They are not necessary for any of the great purposes of commerce, revenue or agriculture,"[11] he said.

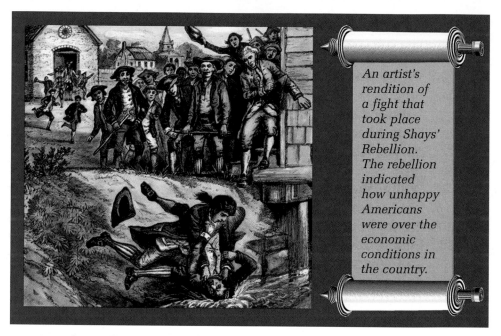

An artist's rendition of a fight that took place during Shays' Rebellion. The rebellion indicated how unhappy Americans were over the economic conditions in the country.

Hamilton then stated his opinion that "the British government was the best in the world."[12]

The convention was stunned. Many of these men had just risked their lives in a war to get America out from under the thumb of the British government. Was Hamilton telling them to bring it back?

Hamilton laid out his governmental plan: two houses, one elected for a three-year term and one with the members picked by electors chosen by the people; an elected judiciary; a chief executive much like the current American president; and departments of finance, war, and foreign affairs.

Hamilton's plan was not well received. On June 29 he left the convention to attend to business in New York. He continued to go back and forth from the convention to New York City throughout July and August as the Constitution was being hammered out. Although it was not what he wanted, Hamilton several times spoke in support of it. It was, he said, "better than nothing."[13]

On the last day of the convention, some delegates were still so opposed to the Constitution that they refused to sign. Greatly agitated, Hamilton said that every member should sign, because even a few non-signers could hurt the chances of ratification. He then signed the document—the only New York delegate to do so.

The Articles of Confederation

Before the Constitution, the Articles of Confederation and Perpetual Union were the law of the land for America.

On July 12, 1776, about a week after the Declaration of Independence was signed, a committee in the Second Continental Congress headed by John Dickinson submitted a draft of the Articles to the full Congress. As first presented, they were much different than they would become. They called for a strong central government with the ability to assess taxes, regulate trade, and perform other functions.

John Dickinson

Since America was fighting against a country with a strong central government (England), there was fear over creating a similar type of government. During months of debate, Congress significantly changed the Articles, giving much more independence and control to the states and severely limiting the power of the central government. The federal government was to be financed by donations from the states based on land values. The revised Articles were finally presented to Congress on November 17, 1777. On March 1, 1781, the Articles went into effect.

The weakness of the Articles quickly became apparent. Congress often did not have the money it needed to operate. The states essentially ignored Congress, sometimes not sending money. Because of a lack of funds, Congress could not pay off America's debts, or even raise an army to defend the country. In addition, states entered trade wars with one another.

Numerous events demonstrated the ineffectivenss of the Articles. One very important event signified the weakness of the Articles. Congress could not get the states to agree to support the Treaty of Paris, which ended the American Revolution. Another obstacle was trying to defend America's borders against the British and Spanish, because the states would not contribute money for an army. Finally, Shays' Rebellion in 1786 and 1787 dramatically emphasized the weakness of the central government. This and other protests, along with criticism of the Articles by many national leaders, led to the Constitutional Convention of 1787, which devised the current U.S. Constitution. The Articles of Confederation were replaced by the Constitution on June 21, 1788, but remained in effect until 1790.

For Your Information

All four of these key figures of the American Revolution attended at least one Continental Congress and then continued in political office. (Left to right) John Adams would become the second president of the United States. Gouverneur Morris, who authored much of the Constitution, would become a minister to France and a senator from New York. Alexander Hamilton would establish the treasury. Thomas Jefferson would become the third president of the United States.

CHAPTER 5

Federalist

Once the proposed Constitution came out of the convention, there was a terrific political fight to get it accepted by a two-thirds majority of the states, or nine of the thirteen that existed then.

As forces in New York mobilized to defeat ratification, Hamilton decided to throw himself into the fight. As one of the largest states, New York's support of the new Constitution was critical. Hamilton conceived of the famous project known historically as the Federalist Papers. The Federalist Papers were a series of newspaper essays supporting the Constitution's adoption.

Initially, the Federalist Papers were supposed to number 25, written by three men who supported the Constitution: Hamilton, James Madison, and John Jay. But Jay developed rheumatism and wrote only five pieces, while Madison was busy as a Congressional delegate from Virginia. Thus most of the writing of what ultimately became 85 essays fell to Hamilton. The writers used the pen name Publius for every one of the Federalist Papers, so it is not certain who wrote which ones. Many historians feel Hamilton wrote at least 51 of the articles, including the first and last ones.

The Federalist Papers were Hamilton's greatest political achievement. He talked to newspaper readers in a very simple manner. In the first article, published on October 27, 1787, Hamilton wrote: "After a full experience of the insufficiency of the existing federal government, you are invited to deliberate upon a new Constitution

for the United States of America. The subject speaks its own importance."[1]

By the time the last Federalist Paper was published at the end of May in 1788, Hamilton had made the case many times for ratifying the Constitution. The new government system, he summarized in the last essay, "may not be perfect in every part [but it] is, upon the whole, a good one."[2]

As Hamilton, Madison, and Jay waged their war of words, other states were ratifying the Constitution. Delaware was first, on December 7, 1787. New Hampshire was the ninth state to ratify it, on June 21, 1788, making it official. But New York's support was still important. On July 26, at a special convention in Poughkeepsie with Hamilton in attendance, New York ratified the Constitution by a vote of 30-27.

Two days later Hamilton returned to New York City. He personally carried the ratified Constitution to Congress. (New York City was the country's capital then.) Before that, however, there had been a massive parade in the city celebrating ratification. At the front of the parade was a ship named *Hamilton.* Everywhere there were eagles and stars, symbols of the new national government. The people cheered Hamilton's name, for they knew he had played a critical role in getting the Constitution ratified. The boy from the West Indies had made it big in America.

George Washington became America's first president under the new Constitution, and he began filling his cabinet posts. Because of the country's shaky financial status, Treasury Secretary was perhaps the most important position. Washington's first choice for the job was Robert Morris, superintendent of finance under the old Articles of Confederation. As the story goes, Washington asked Morris what to do about the public debt, expecting Morris to offer his help. Morris answered: "There is but one man in the United States who can tell you. That is Alexander Hamilton."[3] Thus Hamilton became Washington's choice for Secretary of the Treasury.

On April 30, 1789, Washington was inaugurated. As the first president, everything was new. Washington had many questions: What should he be called? How should he act? Should he entertain? Should he visit private citizens? Hamilton quickly became the president's chief adviser. He was always ready with an answer or an opinion. Washington trusted him because of their wartime experiences.

Robert Morris, who helped finance the Continental Army, served as the country's superintendent of finance from 1781 to 1784. When President Washington asked his help with the new nation's treasury, Morris recommended Alexander Hamilton for the job.

Hamilton wasted little time in proposing new ideas. He had been in office only a month when he advocated the creation of a waterborne military unit to crack down on smuggling and improve tax revenues. (No tax is paid on smuggled goods.) The next summer, Congress approved a Revenue Marine force of ten ships for that purpose. This was the ancestor of the United States Coast Guard. (Hamilton's interest in seagoing military units never wavered. He also played an important part in helping to create the United States Navy, which was established by the Naval Act of 1794.)

During the spring and summer of 1789, Hamilton strengthened his relationship with Angelica Church. She returned to America from England in March, leaving her husband and her children

behind. Hamilton welcomed her with open arms. At first she lived with him and his wife, but that quickly became uncomfortable. Hamilton rented her an apartment nearby.

Angelica was everything Betsy was not. She loved the city and fancy parties, and was knowledgeable about music and literature. She kept up with the political gossip and was friendly, lively, and outgoing. She was very popular with some of the leading men of Hamilton's time, including Thomas Jefferson and John Jay.

On the other hand, Betsy was shy and quiet. She hated the dirty, noisy city. Instead of parties, she liked to do needlepoint. She often took the children to the Albany estate of her parents, many times without Hamilton. At some point during the summer of 1789, some historians feel, Angelica and Hamilton became lovers. Again, the exact relationship between them will probably never be known.

While waiting for Congress to formally approve his nomination as Treasury Secretary, Hamilton got involved with New York City politics. He tried to make sure that Mayor James Duane was not succeeded by any of his political enemies. This brought a warning from the New York attorney general to stay out of city elections. His name was Aaron Burr.

On September 11, 1789, Congress approved Hamilton's nomination as Secretary of the Treasury. He did not have an easy job. The Treasury Department was the largest department in the new federal government, with 500 employees. Not only did Hamilton have to supervise these men, he also had to figure out a way to stop the United States from going bankrupt. Washington's first order to his Treasury Secretary was to design a new financial system for America in just a few months.

What Hamilton produced was an entirely new financial model. His idea was to replace the economy of the United States—one that had "little active debt and moneyed capital"[4]—with one in which the federal government funded the national debt. By doing so, the U.S. would have a high credit rating, be able to keep taxes low, and stimulate foreign investment. To make the change, he wanted the federal government to assume payment of all the existing debt, especially that of the states. This was known as assumption.

One of Hamilton's most important ideas for the American economy was to change it from an agrarian, or farm-based, one to an industrial one, based on factories and machines. A few European countries were beginning to industrialize. Hamilton believed that industrialization was best for America too, but building factories and

machines took money, as would paying workers to run the machines. Hamilton wanted to create a new class of a few people in America who would have most of the money. They would build factories, and America would become industrial.

There were other parts to his economic plan, all of which were interconnected. The failure of one could sink them all. According to a famous story told by Thomas Jefferson, one day in the spring of 1790, Hamilton met Jefferson, the Secretary of State, on the street. Hamilton told Jefferson about his idea of assumption. It faced a rough ride in Congress. Could Jefferson help?

He could. According to Jefferson, on June 20, 1790, Hamilton, Jefferson, and several others met for breakfast at Jefferson's home. At that meeting, Jefferson agreed to provide Congressional votes for Hamilton's plan. In return, Hamilton agreed to support locating the federal government's proposed capital city further south, along the banks of the Potomac River. Hamilton had wanted New York City to remain the nation's capital.

This plan, along with the subsequent creation of a national bank, put America on a firm financial footing both nationally and internationally. Today America is an industrialized country, so many people feel that Hamilton's vision was right. His statue stands in the middle of New York City's mighty financial district, because many people consider him to be the father of America's capitalistic economy.

But Hamilton paid a high price for his "victories" in establishing a new American economy. He made many enemies, including Jefferson and his former Federalist Papers ally James Madison, who both turned against him when they realized the extent to which he was devoted to a strong central government. In addition, both men favored the agricultural economy over the industrial one, and felt that the country was better off as a nation of farmers rather than factory workers. They also did not like his plan for creating a class of a few wealthy Americans, feeling that it was undemocratic.

The three also differed over Hamilton's interpretation of the clause "necessary and proper" in the Constitution. Jefferson and Madison argued since the Constitution did not specifically mention the creation of a national bank, the bank was unconstitutional. Hamilton, however, said that the Constitution gave the government the power to take all "necessary and proper" actions, and the bank fell under that category.

By taking that view, Hamilton assured that the Constitution would not quickly become outdated. Frequently over the years the government has taken many actions not specifically named in the Constitution, but which have been considered "necessary and proper."

Perhaps it was the strain of all the political battles he fought that made Hamilton fall for the tearful story of Maria Reynolds in July 1791. The pretty woman came to Hamilton, sobbing that her husband had left her and her daughter all alone in New York City. Could he help her?

"A pretty woman in distress,"[5] Hamilton described her. The two began an affair. But suddenly in December 1791, Reynolds' husband James returned. It became obvious that he intended to blackmail Hamilton. Fearful of being exposed, Hamilton paid out $1,750 to James Reynolds by August 1792. However, he continued to see Maria.

By late fall 1792, James Reynolds was in jail and claiming that Hamilton had misused government money. Three congressmen, including future President James Monroe, went to Hamilton to confront him with the charges. They quickly realized, however, that the Reynolds matter was personal rather than public, and were convinced that he had not committed any wrong. Still, as word spread about the affair, Hamilton's reputation tumbled.

(Eventually Maria divorced her husband. Her divorce lawyer was Aaron Burr.)

By this point Hamilton and Jefferson were regularly locking horns in Cabinet meetings. (The two were "like pitted cocks,"[6] Jefferson said.) The two sides were splitting into political parties. Those who favored Hamilton's ideas were called Federalists, and those who followed Jefferson were called Republicans (which later became the Democratic Party). The French Revolution only made the differences between the two groups sharper. Republicans favored the French, while Federalists were horrified by the bloody violence sweeping the streets of Paris.

Jefferson pointed out that France had helped America in its revolution. Should Americans not return the favor? Besides, the U.S. had treaties of amity and commerce with France. Was America not duty-bound to honor them?

Other European countries, including England, had declared war against France. Hamilton pointed out that a vast majority of America's trade was with Great Britain. A war against them could be crippling economically. Besides, the French government that had

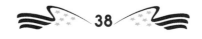

James Monroe, who would become the fifth president of the United States, was on the committee to investigate whether Alexander Hamilton had used government money to pay a blackmailer. Hamilton was found not guilty of the charge.

helped America and with whom treaties were signed—that of King Louis XVI—was gone. The king was dead. In his place was a chaotic government that seemed to change monthly. Hamilton thought it was best to steer clear of France.

On and on the two men fought, with Washington in the middle. Finally Jefferson, weary of the fighting, left the cabinet in December 1793.

When Hamilton's friend and former Assistant Secretary of the Treasury William Duer was involved in a scandal in 1792, it gave Hamilton's enemies more opportunities to attack him. Five resolutions were introduced in Congress, alleging inappropriate behavior by Hamilton as Treasury Secretary. All were defeated after Hamilton provided proof of his innocence.

On January 31, 1795, Hamilton left his post as Secretary of the Treasury. He could feel proud that he was leaving the young nation on a firm financial footing. His policies had solved America's immediate financial crisis. Better yet, he had set the country on a long-term course to economic strength and prosperity.

Hamilton added to his list of enemies in 1796. He worked behind the scenes to have Federalist candidate Thomas Pinckney, and not John Adams, elected as president after Washington. Adams narrowly won the election, but his wife, Abigail, was furious at Hamilton.

"As great a hypocrite as any in the U.S.,"[7] she called him.

Hamilton was soon to face far worse. In the summer of 1797, he was forced to publicly admit the entire affair with Maria Reynolds so that public confidence in the treasury and in his financial system would remain strong. He wrote and printed a pamphlet containing a detailed account of the affair to prove his involvement to be nothing more than bad personal judgment. The writing and publishing of the pamphlet was seen by many as a great mistake on Hamilton's part. (Madison cited "the ingenious folly of its author."[8]) Even though he was guilty of no political wrong, he brought great embarrassment and shame to both him and his wife. It was as if he was saying that his political reputation was more important to him than his personal reputation. Meanwhile, the public confession did not help him much with either side. Republicans still believed he was guilty of wrongdoing. Federalists were concerned that his sinking reputation was hurting them.

A little-known result of the Reynolds affair was that Hamilton asked Monroe to write that he had dropped the investigation of the affair several years before because he believed Hamilton to be innocent. When Monroe refused, Hamilton challenged him to a duel. Monroe's second in the duel was Aaron Burr. Although the duel was never fought, Hamilton came away from the experience hating both Monroe and Burr.

On December 14, 1799, Hamilton received another blow when George Washington, the man who had been his strongest political ally, died. "He was an aegis [protector] very essential to me," Hamilton admitted.[9]

In early May 1800, the Republicans captured control of the New York legislature. This distressed Hamilton, because it meant that the Republican candidate in the upcoming presidential election would win the legislature's support. Worse, everyone credited his enemy, Aaron Burr, with guiding the Republicans to victory.

That year Hamilton made another political error when he opposed the reelection of John Adams. Adams and Hamilton were both Federalists. By opposing Adams, Hamilton destroyed the Federalist Party. It never won another presidential election. Because of his actions, Hamilton was seen, said his friend Robert Troup, "as an unfit head of the party."[10]

Others also wondered why Hamilton did what he did to Adams. Federalist Noah Webster said, "Your conduct on this occasion will be deemed little short of insanity."[11]

The presidential election of 1800 ended in a tie between Thomas Jefferson and Aaron Burr. The House of Representatives had to vote to break the tie. Once again Hamilton worked behind the scenes, this time to deny the election to his hated enemy Burr. He succeeded, and Jefferson became president.

November 1801 brought Hamilton's greatest tragedy. His eldest son Philip, just nineteen years old, was killed in a duel. (The exact date of his death has been given as the 21st, 22nd, or 23rd.) The boy was his father's favorite. Hamilton considered Philip as the family's "eldest and brightest hope."[12] His senseless death caused Hamilton's seventeen-year-old daughter Angelica to suffer a mental breakdown. For the rest of her life she remained childlike, and talked about Philip as if he were still alive.

The death of Philip sent Hamilton into a deep depression. "Never did I see a man so completely overwhelmed with grief as Hamilton has been,"[13] wrote an observer. Hamilton himself, writing a few months later, revealed: "Every day proves to me more and more that this American world was not made for me."[14]

No longer considered the leader of the Federalists, Hamilton had become a has-been. He silently watched his old enemy Thomas Jefferson become a popular president. Ironically, the act that sealed his popularity was the Louisiana Purchase in April 1803. To justify its constitutionality, Jefferson cited the "necessary and proper" reasoning that Hamilton had conceived, and to which Jefferson had been so opposed.

In the spring of 1804, Aaron Burr, still vice president but knowing that Jefferson and his party did not want him, ran for governor of New York. He lost badly, in part because Hamilton worked against him in the election. Burr knew that Hamilton had denied him the presidency in 1800. Now he added the governor's race to his list of grievances.

For his part, Hamilton was discouraged over his lost political standing, and he was still depressed over the death of Philip. This was his state of mind as he went to fight the duel with Aaron Burr on July 11, 1804—the duel that sent him, seriously wounded, on his way back to New York a short time later. . . .

Alexander Hamilton did not survive his duel with Burr. After much suffering, he died the next day, Thursday, July 12, 1804. He was forty-nine years old.

Historians have debated for years whether or not Hamilton intended to shoot Burr. Some say that because Hamilton had repeatedly announced his intention to fire into the air, he did not try to shoot Burr. They feel that the depressed Hamilton went to the duel hoping to be killed. In a way, they feel that Hamilton committed suicide.

Others, however, differ. They say that if Hamilton did not intend to shoot at Burr, why did he put on spectacles? Why did he test the light? They also point out that Hamilton made work plans for after the duel. They say that this is hardly the action of a man who wanted to die. They also say that his actions and words before the duel show that he was definitely not in a suicidal state of mind.

The pistols that were used were the same set, ironically, that Philip Hamilton had used three years earlier. The one Hamilton used had a special hair-trigger mechanism so that it could be fired easily. Historically, the story has been that Hamilton deliberately fired into the air. But what if he set the hair-trigger mechanism secretly, then accidentally shot over Burr's head, causing Burr to then fire at him? Did Hamilton outsmart himself?

Hamilton's death ended any way of discovering the truth.

The duel also ended the political career of Aaron Burr, as Hamilton knew it would. Burr is remembered historically only as the man who killed Alexander Hamilton. His reputation is as a scoundrel and a murderer.

Hamilton, however, is held in very high regard. The duel restored to Hamilton the glory and reputation that he had once enjoyed. Even Burr's own family held Hamilton in awe. Once, soon after the duel, Burr's Aunt Rhoda said to him, "[Y]ou killed that great and good man, Colonel Hamilton."[15]

Somewhere, Alexander Hamilton must have been smiling.

The Society for Establishing Useful Manufactures

Marquis de Lafayette

In July 1778, in the middle of the American Revolution, four men fighting for the Continental Army stopped for a picnic at the Passaic Falls in New Jersey. The four were George Washington, the Marquis de Lafayette, his aide James McHenry, and Alexander Hamilton. Although the men's visit that day was brief, the memory it left with Hamilton was long indeed.

Years later, when Secretary of the Treasury Hamilton was seeking a site to promote his ideas of industrialization in America, he remembered the water power that the thundering waterfalls provided. He chose the Passaic Falls as the site of his experiment, and in so doing founded a new city.

Like many of his ideas, his plans this time were bold. He wanted the federal government to spend $1 million to build an industrial complex run by a group called the Society for Establishing Useful Manufactures (SUM).

Congress turned down the scheme, so Hamilton turned to the private sector. He had New Jersey Governor William Paterson guide it through the state legislature. The new industrial town, named Paterson, was financed by the sale of $600,000 worth of stock.

But bad luck doomed Hamilton's vision. Pierre L'Enfant—the same man who designed Washington, D.C.—was hired to plan Paterson. His elaborate ideas were too costly, and he was dismissed. In an economic downturn, many SUM stockholders lost money. Another problem was that it was difficult to find skilled workers to run the machines. Facing these and other obstacles, in 1796 the SUM gave up. Only two factories were built: a four-story cotton mill and a smaller building used for bleaching and printing.

Ironically, in later years, the city of Paterson would grow to become an economic industrial giant—exactly as Hamilton had envisioned. He had the right idea, but the wrong time.

For Your Information

Chronology

1755 or 1757	Born on island of Nevis, British West Indies
1768	Mother dies
1772	Sails to America
1773	Enters King's College (Columbia University)
1775	Meets George Washington for first time
1776	Becomes Captain of Provincial Company of Artillery; fights in Battle of Trenton
1777	Joins Washington's Staff
1780	Marries Elizabeth Schuyler
1781	Resigns from Washington's staff
1782	Son Philip born
1783	Negotiates with Congress for veterans' payments; sets up law practice
1784	Daughter Angelica born
1785	With Hercules Mulligan, establishes the Society for Promoting the Manumission of Slaves in New York
1786	Son Alexander born
1787	Attends Constitutional Convention in Philadelphia; publishes first Federalist Paper
1788	Son James born
1789	Appointed Secretary of Treasury
1792	Son John born
1795	Resigns as Treasury Secretary
1797	Son William born
1799	Father dies; daughter Eliza born
1801	Helps make Thomas Jefferson President; son Philip killed in duel
1804	Mortally wounded by Aaron Burr at Weehawken, New Jersey

Timeline in History

1705	Edmond Halley predicts the frequency of visits by a comet, now called Halley's comet.
1707	England, Scotland, and Wales unite to create Great Britain.
1714	Britain's Queen Anne dies.
1718	New Orleans is founded.
1725	Peter the Great dies.
1727	Sir Isaac Newton dies.
1731	Benjamin Franklin begins a circulating library in Philadelphia.
1752	Benjamin Franklin experiments with a kite and lightning.
1759	George Washington marries Martha Custis.
1762	The first St. Patrick's Day Parade in New York City is held.
1770	Five people are killed and six wounded by the British at the Boston Massacre.
1773	Patriots dump 342 chests of tea into Boston Harbor at the Boston Tea Party.
1775	The American Revolution starts with the battles of Lexington and Concord.
1776	The Declaration of Independence is issued.
1781	Cornwallis surrenders to Washington at Yorktown.
1789	The French Revolution begins.
1790	The first lifeboat is tested at sea.
1796	George Washington delivers his farewell address.
1799	George Washington dies.
1803	The U.S. purchases Louisiana from the French.
1807	Robert E. Lee is born.
1809	Abraham Lincoln is born.
1812	War breaks out between the United States and Britain over sea rights.
1815	Napoléon Bonaparte is defeated at Waterloo.
1818	Mary Shelley writes *Frankenstein.*
1827	Ludwig van Beethoven dies.
1828	Noah Webster publishes *An American Dictionary of the English Language.*
1836	Texas gains independence from Mexico.
1837	Samuel Morse patents the telegraph.
1845	Edgar Allan Poe writes "The Raven."
1846	The Smithsonian Institution is established.
1847	Thomas A. Edison is born.
1848	Gold is discovered in California.

Chapter Notes

Chapter One: Duel at Dawn

1. Arnold A. Rogow, *A Fatal Friendship* (New York: Hill and Wang, 1998), p. 3.
2. Willard Sterne Randall, *Alexander Hamilton: A Life* (New York: HarperCollins, 2003), p. 2.
3. Ibid.
4. Rogow, p. 247.
5. Randall, p. 2.

Chapter Two: A Boy Alone

1. Willard Sterne Randall, *Alexander Hamilton: A Life* (New York: HarperCollins, 2003), p. 94.

Chapter Three: Washington's Right Hand

1. Willard Sterne Randall, *Alexander Hamilton: A Life* (New York: HarperCollins, 2003), p. 114.
2. Ibid., p. 167.
3. Ibid., p. 165.
4. Ibid., p. 172.
5. Ibid., p. 194.
6. Arnold A. Rogow, *A Fatal Friendship* (New York: Hill and Wang, 1998), p. 58.
7. Ron Chernow, *Alexander Hamilton* (New York: The Penguin Press, 2004), p. 145.
8. Randall, p. 223.
9. Ibid.

Chapter Four: Constitutional Advocate

1. Willard Sterne Randall, *Alexander Hamilton: A Life* (New York: HarperCollins, 2003), p. 233.
2. Ibid., p. 236.
3. Ibid., p. 280.
4. Ibid., p. 292.

5. Ibid., p. 315.
6. Ibid., p. 319.
7. Ibid., p. 327.
8. Ibid., p. 334.
9. Arnold A. Rogow, *A Fatal Friendship* (New York: Hill and Wang, 1998), p. 115.
10. Randall, p. 335.
11. Ibid.
12. Ibid.
13. Ibid., p. 340.

Chapter Five: Federalist

1. Willard Sterne Randall, *Alexander Hamilton: A Life* (New York: HarperCollins, 2003), p. 346.
2. Ibid., p. 348.
3. Ibid., p. 361.
4. Ibid., pg. 388.
5. Ibid., p. 406.
6. Donald Barr Chidsey, *Mr. Hamilton and Mr. Jefferson* (Nashville, Tennessee: Thomas Nelson Inc., 1975), p. 25.
7. Arnold A. Rogow, *A Fatal Friendship* (New York, Hill and Wang, 1998), p. 165.
8. Ibid., p. 153.
9. Randall, p. 422.
10. Rogow, p. 293.
11. Ibid., p. 295.
12. Ron Chernow, *Alexander Hamilton* (New York, The Penguin Press, 2004), p. 651.
13. Ibid., p. 655.
14. Ibid., p. 658.
15. Ibid., p. 721.

Further Reading

For Young Adults

Collier, James Lincoln. *The Alexander Hamilton You Never Knew.* New York: Children's Press, 2003.

DeCarolis, Lisa. *Alexander Hamilton: Federalist and Founding Father.* New York: Rosen Publishing Group, 2003.

Haugen, Brenda. *Alexander Hamilton: Founding Father and Statesman.* Minneapolis: Compass Point Books, 2005.

Jones, Veda Boyd. *Alexander Hamilton.* Philadelphia: Chelsea House, 1999.

Rosenberg, Pam. *Alexander Hamilton: Soldier and Statesman.* Chanhassen, Minnesota: Child's World, 2004.

Whitelaw, Nancy. *A More Perfect Union: The Story of Alexander Hamilton.* Greensboro, N.C.: Morgan Reynolds, 1997.

Works Consulted

Chernow, Ron. *Alexander Hamilton.* New York: The Penguin Press, 2004.

Chidsey, Donald Barr. *Mr. Hamilton and Mr. Jefferson.* Nashville, Tennessee: Thomas Nelson, Inc., 1975.

Duel. Hamilton vs. Burr with Richard Dreyfuss [video recording] / produced by Richard Dreyfuss and Lynn Falcon for History Television Network Productions; written by Chris Intaglinta, Richard Dreyfuss; directed by Lynn Falcon.Burlington, VT : A&E Television Networks; New York: Distributed by New Video, 2004.

Kennedy, Roger G. *Burr, Hamilton, and Jefferson: A Study in Character.* New York: Oxford University Press, 2000.

Randall, Willard Sterne. *Alexander Hamilton: A Life.* New York: HarperCollins, 2003.

Rogow, Arnold A. *A Fatal Friendship: Alexander Hamilton and Aaron Burr.* New York: Hill and Wang, 1998.

On the Internet

Alexander Hamilton—Free Online Library
http://hamilton.thefreelibrary.com

Alexander Hamilton | The New-York Historical Society
http://www.alexanderhamiltonexhibition.org

Archiving Early America
http://www.earlyamerica.com

Index